Together in Trust

Together in Trust

Twenty-four Select Wedding Meditations

HORACE BROWN KING

C.S.S. Publishing Co.
Lima, Ohio

TOGETHER IN TRUST

LIBRARY OF CONGRESS
Library of Congress Cataloging-in-Publication Data

King, Horace Brown, 1943-
Together in trust: twenty-four select wedding meditations / Horace Brown King.
p. cm.
ISBN 1-556-73108-6
1. Wedding sermons. 2. Marriage — Sermons. 3. United Methodist Church (U.S.) — Sermons. 4. Methodist Church — Sermons. 5. Sermons, American. I. Title.
BV4278.K55 1989 88-23387
252'.1—dc 19 CIP

9819 / ISBN 1-55673-108-6 PRINTED IN U.S.A.

Table of Contents

About the Author

Horace Brown King was born in Lewisburg, Pennsylvania, on November 1, 1943, and grew up in Dalton, Pennsylvania, where he was confirmed in the Methodist Church.

Undergraduate work was pursued at Mansfield University, and resulted in a degree in Music Education. A call to full-time ministry was also received while at Mansfield, but was deferred until after a year of graduate study at Miami University of Ohio. While at Miami, he was a graduate assistant in Music Theory.

Drew University was selected as seminary, and yielded both the M. Div. and D. Min. degrees. While at seminary, he served the Clifford and Lenoxville United Methodist Churches, and later pastored Embury Church in Scranton; Firwood Church of Wilkes-Barre (all in Pennsylvania); and Waverly United Methodist Church in New York.

Dr. King has served the Wyoming Conference by chairing committees in Education and Communication, while participating as a member of many others. Civic interests include Boy Scouts, the Red Cross, and the United Way. He has sung with many choral groups, some of which he has helped direct. Other interests include reading, travel, genealogy, drama, and Plantagenet history.

Then the Lord God said, "It is not good that the man should be alone; I will make him a helper fit for him."

(Genesis 2:18)

Genesis 2:18 | *Getting Help*

John Lennon coded it right when he wrote about the process of maturity:

When I was younger, so much younger than today,
I never needed anybody else's help in any way . . .

There is a period of time in early adulthood when the world is glorious, each day is Spring, and all that is comes to us for wisdom and counsel.

I suspect that each of us needs to go through such a span of self-sufficiency. This sort of thing encourages us to make and carry out decisions for living. It also keeps us humble and adds to our wisdom when our wonderful skills and ideas get shot full of holes.

Everyone should be a dreamer. And everyone should have at least a few dreams fail.

The Book of Genesis, the Book of Beginnings, is important in its demonstration of God's Wisdom. God's Wisdom is shown in Adam, who wasn't made a robot, but was endowed with the capacity to make mistakes and learn from them.

In Adam, God built all our capacities to plan and hope, our proclivity to take matters into our own limited understanding — and to fall on our faces. It was necessary for Adam to be all these things in order that we descendants might gain a bit of Wisdom!

God created Adam out of his own loneliness — and, after solitude was savored, said, "It is not good for the man to be alone. I will provide a partner for him." The story goes on to tell about all the created beings coming by Adam to see if he'd choose them for his partner. (I know a lady whose T-shirt reads, "The more

I see of men, the more I love my dog!") But Adam, open and innocent as he was, found none of the animals quite right for partnership.

Thus God made some manipulations, and the first woman came into Being. The story concludes, "That is why a man leaves his father and mother and is united to his wife, and the two become one flesh." Not only did God allow for loneliness, but garnished that loneliness with partnership!

The Wisdom of the Bible keeps reminding us that humans are in the process of moving from slavery to freedom, from promise into fulfillment, from solitude into community and companionship.

John Lennon's song goes on to remind us that, as years and experiences increase, we find that we *do* need help — and cry out for it. There's nothing wrong with that.

__________ and __________, you've come here this afternoon because you've realized that you need a partner. I personally like the translation of the biblical word as "partner" more than "helpmate," although they do mean the same thing. But "partner" implies a needed level of sharing, where neither one is necessarily in charge all the time.

In a partnership, each does what he or she does best — not only for self, but for the other as well. Partners are those who can agree on what needs to be done and how best to do it. Partnerships become wobbly when one or the other decides that he or she needs no other help, and thus tries to do everything.

__________ and __________, you've not jumped into this partnership cold. You've given a lot of thought and planning as to who does what, how and where to live, and what the merger will look like in ten to twenty years. In the midst of these well-made dreams, you need to realize that there's *another* partner involved: God, who created Adam and Eve as partners, has created them to be *his* partners as well.

There'll be times when your combined wisdom just won't be enough.

There'll be times when you may feel scared, confronted by panic.

Your earthly partner may have times of illness, or a need for solitude.

I've heard of some families where one partner actually became grumpy with the other!

In all of it, God loves you, and will be a *steadfast* partner. And if he's steadfast to you, you each can be steadfast with each other. As you celebrate your love today, celebrate also your God-given partnership.

They go together, each deepening the other.

So, let your individual lives merge with each other, making for a deep and loving partnership — which is what God wants you to do!

Then the man said, "This at last is bone of my bones and flesh of my flesh; she shall be called Woman, because she was taken out of Man."

Therefore a man leaves his father and his mother and cleaves to his wife, and they become one flesh.

(Genesis 2:23-24)

Genesis 2:23-24 | *Now This, At Last*

A young, attractive woman reporter named Terry was sent by *Life* magazine to do a feature story on the jungles of of the Amazon. She was not heard from for over a year. Fearing the worst, a macho Indiana Jones-type fellow was sent to track her down. He forded wild rivers and jumped terrifying waterfalls. He fought off mosquitoes and gnats, and suffered from the intense heat of the tropics. But he finally stumbled into an Indian village, where his reporter was honored as a queen. Bowing low, he doffed his safari-hat and gallantly exclaimed, "Ah, sweet Ms. Terry of *Life*, at last I've found you."

One of the mysteries of life is finding a suitable partner. The Creator, in his wisdom, saw that it wasn't good to be alone. After all, he himself had created out of a longing. And so he created various species of animal and bird, to let the first human name them. And though Adam named them well, he could find none which was entirely satisfactory as a partner.

> *And so the Lord God put the man into a trance, and while he slept, he took one of his ribs and closed the flesh over the place. The Lord God then built up the rib, which he had taken out of the man, into a woman. He brought her to the man, and the man said: "Now this, at last — bone from my bones, flesh from my flesh! — this shall be called woman, for from man was this taken."*

And that's why a man leaves his parents and his old, familiar surroundings, and becomes partners with his wife.

__________ and __________, this is an old and oft-told story, and you know it well. I remind you of it today to impress upon you how important it is to have an adequate partner. It's more fashionable at weddings to talk about love and lace, promises and perspectives. And we should. But the core of lasting marriage is *partnership*, the concept of being a team, the giving of the *self* in order that the *other* shall also profit.

Partnership doesn't mean putting your own candle out, for that would lessen the warmth. But it *does* imply a joining together of the unique personalities you each bring to this marriage.

__________ and __________, you are here before us today to make public that at last you have found a suitable partner! By doing so, you are helping each of us either to refine our own partnerships or to understand better what we individually seek in a companion.

The one who recorded the Creation Story in human language identifies this first partnership as conceived in a trance — and there are times in each partnership when we also wonder . . . That's only natural. But whatever ribbing we choose to give the other, we can yet affirm that flesh and bone belong together according to God's plan.

Dear friends, live in love. Give to each other comfort, cheer and honor — and a shoulder for the times of grief. But most of all, be worthy partners.

You have joined your hands together in trust and sharing: help the rest of us to see how God's gift of partnership can be!

"All the commandment which I command you this day you shall be careful to do, that you may live and multiply, and go in and possess the land which the Lord swore to give to your fathers. And you shall remember all the way which the Lord your God has led you these forty years in the wilderness, that he might humble you, testing you to know what was in your heart, whether you would keep his commandments, or not. And he humbled you and let you hunger and fed you with manna, which you did not know, nor did your fathers know; that he might make you know that man does not live by bread alone, but that man lives by everything that proceeds out of the mouth of the Lord. Your clothing did not wear out upon you, and your foot did not swell, these forty years. Know then in your heart that, as a man disciplines his son, the Lord your God is bringing you into a good land, a land of brooks of water, of fountains and springs, flowing forth in valleys and hills, a land of wheat and barley, of vines and fig trees and pomegranates, a land of olive trees and honey, a land in which you will eat bread without scarcity, in which you will lack nothing, a land whose stones are iron, and out of whose hills you can dig copper. And you shall eat and be full, and you shall bless the Lord your God for the good land he has given you.

Take heed lest you forget the Lord your God, by not keeping his commandments and his ordinances and his statutes, which I command you this day: lest, when you have eaten and are full, and have built goodly houses and live in them, and when your herds and flocks multiply, and your silver and gold is multiplied, and all that you have is multiplied, then your heart be lifted up, and you forget the Lord your God, who brought you out of the land of Egypt, out of the house of bondage, who led you through the great and terrible wilderness, with its fiery serpents and scorpions and thirsty ground where there was no water, who brought you water out of the flinty rock, who fed you in the wilderness with manna which your fathers did not know, that he might humble you and test you, to do you good in the end. Beware lest you say in your heart, 'My power and the might of my hand have gotten me this wealth.' You shall remember the Lord your God, for it is he who gives you power to get wealth; that he may confirm his covenant which he swore to your fathers, as at this day.

(Deuteronomy 8:1-18)

Deuteronomy 8:1-18

The Right Stuff

The Right Stuff is a movie that'll space you out. It's about the American astronauts, pioneers of the heavens, those heroes who've risked the perils of a hard journey to prove that it could be done.

But the movie isn't all heroics. It provides some personal glimpses into the personalities of the astronauts and their families, those who try and succeed, those who try and fall short.

The Right Stuff is a little too glorious for some viewers, and some have accused it of being a political vehicle. Yet here is an examination of the hopes and the anguish of ordinary, quiet heroes who dare hitch their wagon to a star.

Perhaps that's what "getting hitched" is all about! Those who use this quaint term for marriage have given us an image of attachment which is hard to surpass. We "get hitched" to each other, certainly; and also to a higher ideal which surpasses our earthly framework and allows us to pass freely along the lines of the cosmos.

To really overdo the analogy, we could have our soloist sing, "Fly Me to the Moon"!

The ancient people of Israel sought also the new and better horizon. Under the leadership of Moses, they escaped the cruel slavery of the Prince of Egypt and started out once again for the Promised Land.

The scribe of the Book of Deuteronomy records God's Word spoken to his people through Moses. He reminds the wanderers that, although the desert can be difficult, the Land Beyond is worth the trip.

He also affirms that he, the Lord, has been and will be with them:

- to humble them and thus exalt them;
- to bring them to a place of hunger and thirst in order that he may provide for them;
- to show them that under his care their lives and possessions should prosper.

And the Promise is worth the Pilgrimage!

For the Lord your God is bringing you to a rich land, a land of streams, of springs and underground waters gushing out in hill and valley . . . You will have plenty to eat and will bless the Lord your God for the rich land that he has given you.

If the people of Israel adhere to the Lord, he says, they will indeed be recipients of "the right stuff."

__________ and __________, these can be words for your journey. The Promise is worth the Pilgrimage! It is good not to dwell in the desert, but to remember how it was when you sojourned there. And I cannot, in all honesty, stand before you to say that your ritual of Marriage is the arrival of the Promised Land! For there are yet rivers with deep currents of emotion, the rocky paths of jealousy and the tempting spas of independence to overcome and pass. But the Word of the Lord that led his People out of Egypt's dehumanization is likewise available to lead you through the transitions.

__________ and __________, your presence here and the substance of this ceremony indicates to us that you see each other as bearers of "the right stuff." It's our sincere wish for you that you may always perceive the hope of this day, that you may look beyond the spacial pressures of the Trip Together into the qualities which have sent you on the journey.

In all places, bear our love and that of each other.

And remember the Lord your God. It is he that gives you strength to become prosperous, so fulfilling the covenant guaranteed by oath with your forefathers, as he is doing now.

O sing to the Lord a new song,
for he has done marvelous things!
His right hand and his holy arm
have gotten him victory.
The Lord has made known his victory.
He has revealed his vindication
in the sight of the nations.
He has remembered his steadfast
love and faithfulness
to the house of Israel.
All the ends of the earth have seen
the victory of our God.

Make a joyful noise to the Lord,
all the earth;
break forth into joyous song
and sing praises!
Sing praises to the Lord with the lyre,
with the lyre and the sound of melody!
With trumpets and the sound of the horn
make a joyful noise before the
King, the Lord!

Let the sea roar, and all that fills
it;
the world and those who dwell
in it!
Let the floods clap their hands;
let the hills sing for joy
together
before the Lord, for he comes
to judge the earth.
He will judge the world with
righteousness,
and the peoples with equity.

(Psalm 98)

Psalm 98 | *A New Song*

Baroque music is really my favorite.

I enjoy the moving counterpoint, the stretching bass, the massive choirs. For me, there's nothing as contemplative and quieting as an evening with Vivaldi or Corelli or one of these old masters.

But every once in a while I want to hear some *new* music, as well. It comes at me from MTV, or the radio, or even from the health spas. The music of the air is always new music. The songs we whistled last year are now heard only on collections called "The Best of '84," sold exclusively on late-night TV, records or cassettes.

Music fades fast.

Not long ago, one of my kids asked me if I could remember the Beatles . . .

The God whom we worship is a contemporary God, a God of newness. The New Song which we sing to the Lord honors him and celebrates his wonderful things. Although the people of Israel ran off after strange gods and foreign lovers, our Lord kept his promise to the people of Israel with loyalty and constant love for them. The victory which God claims is that of recalling his own people to him, that of reconciling an estranged group of believers.

It seems fitting that we should be reminded of this on a wedding day! This is a day when age-old vows are exchanged and a brand-new covenant is made. This is a day when families have gathered to see once again the old drama of love's realization played anew before their very eyes.

A wedding celebrates a marriage. And a marriage is a

recognition that, despite our human tendencies to irresponsibly seek out our own pleasures and desires, loyalty and constant love do ultimately prevail!

__________ and __________, you have brought us here today because you have something to tell us. We hear you telling us that together you believe in the now-familiar virtues of love and care, honor and trust and respect. We hear you saying that you'll stick by one another through thick and thin. We hear this song and rejoice, for we've heard it and sung it before. Yet it's a *new* song, because you're singing it for us afresh.

__________ and __________, there'll be times when the harmony sounds weird.

Rehearsals will break down.

Performances may get plastic.

You may get tired of practicing.

And please understand that even if your chords get sour, the Song of God continues to pour its richness over and around you. And as you listen, you'll be able to correct your own singing to join with the Eternal!

Sing for joy to the Lord, all the earth;
praise him with songs and shouts of joy!

And, as you live together under God's blessing, know that the New Song and the Old Song are His Song. And remember that your love is a reminder to us all that God is indeed at work in our lives!

The wolf shall dwell with the
lamb,
and the leopard shall lie down
with the kid,
and the calf and the lion and the
fatling together,
and a little child shall lead
them.
The cow and the bear shall feed;
their young shall lie down
together;
and the lion shall eat straw like
the ox.
The sucking child shall play over
the hole of the asp,
and the weaned child shall put
his hand on the adder's den.
They shall not hurt or destroy
in all my holy mountain;
for the earth shall be full of the
knowledge of the Lord
as the waters cover the sea.

(Isaiah 11:6-9)

Isaiah 11:6-9 | *The Peaceable Kingdom*

Once there was a pet shop which had a beautiful parrot. This parrot had shiny feathers of gorgeous hue, a fine strong beak, and a healthful attitude on life. But the amazing bird wouldn't talk — which considerably lessened his value. One day, the truck which brought the food supplies was late, and the only thing for the parrot to eat was ravioli. But when his cup was set before him, he puffed up his feathers and screeched, "I *hate* ravioli!" The owners and clerks ran over to his perch: "You CAN talk!" they exclaimed. "Of *course* I can talk," snapped the bird, "but up to now, everything was fine!"

There are some of you here who would agree that feeding time at the pet shop is one of noise and confusion. There are some cynics in our midst who may snicker, "Marriage is like feeding time in the pet shop!" The terms we use to describe each other may vary. Some men are described as "animals" or "beasts." Married women have called their husbands "turkeys" or "toads." (I understand that to be called a "tiger" is a horse-of-a-different color!)

Women, also, are named in derogatory fashion as "wildcats" — or just "catty" — or labeled as a "real dog." Some are "vixens," while their younger sisters are just plain foxy! We'd better not monkey with this any more, or it'll get out of hand . . .

The rivalry between animal species, predators and prey, has been long observed and is common knowledge. Yet God originally created all these beasts to like each other, or at least to live with each other in a supportive way. But ungodliness broke up the system — and as Creation fell away from tolerance and unity, competition to the death came in.

The wages of Sin *is* Death.

In the coming days, when God reclaims his Creation which once he pronounced good, jealousy and fear will again be banished. Isaiah looks for this —

Then the wolf shall live with the sheep.
and the leopard lie down with the kid;
the calf and the young lion shall grow up together,
and a little child shall lead them;
the cow and the bear shall be friends,
and their young shall lie down together.
The lion shall eat straw like cattle;
the infant shall play over the hole of the cobra.
and the young child dance over the viper's nest.
They shall not hurt or destroy in all my holy mountain . . .

__________ and __________, you know that it's a jungle out there.

Most of your married friends can tell you that at times, Life Together can be a zoo. But the point of our gathering today is to affirm that marriage *is* possible, despite our natural instincts to devour each other and protect and mark our individual turf!

I honestly believe that God's intent was that his creatures should exist side by side in an ecological and spiritual community. Even though that dream has been wrecked and scarred by our impatience, God has not given up on the dream.

__________ and __________, your marriage is one example of how life can work, the two of you living and working peacefully together, side by side. The commitments you have made to each other defy the old jungle law, and have admitted the possibility of a Peaceable Kingdom. Your marriage is but a small clearing amidst the wild terrain. But we look to you, as you make this work, to help show the rest of us that love triumphs over evil, that patience can heal anger . . .

Thank you for being in love!

Thank you for reminding us of our own love!

And thank you for being one more demonstrable instance that God wills his people to be together!

God bless you.

You shall no more be termed
Forsaken,
and your land shall no more be
termed Desolate;
but you shall be called My delight
is in her,
and your land Married,
for the Lord delights in you,
and your land shall be married.
For as a young man marries a
virgin,
so shall your sons marry you,
and as the bridegroom rejoices
over the bride,
so shall your God rejoice over
you.

(Isaiah 62:4-5)

Isaiah 62:4-5 | *The Beloved Country*

There is a land somewhere which lies within the middle-earth of our fondest imagination, which shines with the hope of Someday even when our immediate moments threaten us.

There's a far country inside our imagination where we can moor our boat away from the daily river and take our respite among the leaves of today and yesterday.

The vista changes as we do.

When we were very young, the Magic Kingdom became a giant amusement park, where the rides never malfunctioned and no evening threatened to dispel our fun. As we grew older, Never-Never Land became filled with adventure: either pirates to conquer or corporations to subdue, Indians and alligators or romance and recognition.

Beyond these times, our Land of Somewhere has become more pastoral: the Quiet Life prevails, the old ways of family, friends and long evenings carry us forward with their promise crouching just beyond Tomorrow's doorstep . . . We all have a Land — of hope, of glory.

You shall no more be termed Forsaken,
and your land shall no more be termed Desolate;
but you shall be called My Delight is in you,
and your land Married;
for the Lord delights in you,
and your land shall be married.
For as a young man and woman wed one another,
so shall you wed the Lord who rebuilds you,
and your God shall rejoice over you as a bridegroom
and bride rejoice over each other.

Isaiah's message came to a small remnant of Jewish people who had chosen the hard road of returning to Jerusalem after seventy years in Babylon. The city was destroyed, the temple a pile of rubble. The land of their grandfathers' dreams was choked with ruins of the old way. Yet the power of God at work in his covenant people promised to shine forth as a blazing torch to renew the land, to reclaim the dream! What some saw to be Forsaken and Desolate was foretold to be God's Delight, and Married. Wedding the dream to the God who makes it happen is as good as having it right now, for he rejoices in the promise of what is to come. We dare approach the real horizons of the beloved country.

__________ and __________, you've called us here today because you've glimpsed a special country within the relationship which you now have. More, you've asked us to be with you as you joyfully set sail. We who are your fellow-exiles in a profane city of cynic despair celebrate your voyage, for you go in our name.

We're heartened to see willing explorers to a place we also have glimpsed.

Having outfitted several similar expeditions, I won't kid you — there really *are* demons and dragons out there, sea-monsters of chaos and instability, green-eyed griffins of jealousy and frustration. There will be times when you're not sure who's captain and who's mate. You'll need to constantly check your ship for leaks.

But, __________ and __________, the trip is worth it! Trusting in God and trusting in each other, you'll find that the Beloved Country is closer each day.

The covenant you are making this day is that which will continue to define your hopes and reinforce your goals.

The covenant before God assures you of his Presence, as he cares for and nurtures and comforts all his children.

And the covenant before us, your friends, enlists us in the quest as we support you with our prayers and symbols of love.

We encourage you in your journey.

We'd like you to tell us occasionally what your special land looks like.

Plan to stay within that country, for it shall no more be termed Desolate — and accept God's rejoicing, as you rejoice over each other and over your refined image.

God bless you.

(With thanks to Jackie Sabath in *Sojourners*)

You are the light of the world. A city set on a hill cannot be hid. Nor do men light a lamp and put it under a bushel, but on a stand, and it gives light to all in the house. Let your light so shine before men, that they may see your good works and give glory to your Father who is in heaven.

(Matthew 5:14-16)

Matthew 5:14-16 | *A Hole In the Day*

Earlier this morning, as I was struggling against the day, I became increasingly aware that something unpleasant was poking me in the eye. I soon came to realize that the hallway light was on, and there was no escaping its brightness. No matter where I put my bed or my pillow, the hallway light relentlessly pursues and finds me! Even in broad daylight I can be accosted by the hallway light.

When I was little, if I accidentally left a light on, my Pennsylvania Dutch mother would tell me that I was "burning a hole in the day." I've always tried to avoid that — but invariably a light does get left on, perhaps affecting those who aren't expecting to see it there.

Our Lord had some poignant things to say about lighting lights. He told us, through his disciples, that those who believe are bright spots for a whole world which stumbles about and curses the darkness. He says that lamps are not tucked away somewhere but rather set in prominent and strategic places, in order that the dingiest corner can receive a bit of brightness.

> *In the same way your light must shine before people, so that they will see the good things you do and praise your Father in heaven.*

One of the possible good things to do is to affirm our loves before a jaded public. We've heard the horror-stories of abuse and misunderstanding. We've quietly cried in the face of broken dreams. We've changed the channel when marriages have dried up in the heat of the desert. Yet Love is the basic fuel for the light of the world — and in proclaiming love, we once again send a hopeful foray into the teeth of despair.

__________ and __________, you've come here today to vow your love to each other. We, your family and friends, proclaim you our champions, today. For you have picked up the challenge, pulled the switch, and lit the world!

Not only have you lit up each other's life, giving strength to carry on, you have lit up *our* lives as well! You're saying to us, "We've dared to love; now *you* can also."

But, __________ and __________, I have to tell you: There will be days when the darkness is so thick that it's hard to find the lightswitch. Some days you'll be tempted to just disconnect everything and pray for the sunrise. Some days you'll have to change the bulb.

In any and all of these, you have both the Master Power of God and the good services of your friends. Neither wishes you to grope in blackness when such a potent light is at hand! And so we expect you to expect yourselves to be like light for the whole world, agleam with love as Times Square on a rainy evening. Please understand that you have God's love and our best wishes.

Let the light shine!

And don't worry about burning a hole in the day.

You are the light of the world. A city set on a hill cannot be hid. Nor do men light a lamp and put it under a bushel, but on a stand, and it gives light to all in the house. Let your light so shine before men, that they may see your good works and give glory to your Father who is in heaven.

(Matthew 5:14-16)

Matthew 5:14-16 | *Lighting Lives*

It's been a while since Debbie Boone sang "You Light Up My Life." But it has been sung, played and lived out many times since. Persons of singular darkness have suddenly met one whose very person makes the room glow, whose smile spontaneously sparks an avalanche of song. We've all had — or will have — the experience. These good vibes are the very life-blood of our days.

It's an interesting thing: with light comes responsibility. We're required to turn on that charming light, and not to hide it. This deals with sensitivity, I suppose. A person of light needs to realize that someone wants to *receive* that light. Lighting lives expects a certain amount of creative listening — a sense of knowing what and where the Other is — and a willingness to share the specialness of the moment, to make each moment special.

Our Lord spoke of that kind of awareness:

> *No one lights a lamp and puts it under a bowl; instead he puts it on the lampstand, where it gives light for everyone in the house.*

Marriage is quite a bit like this. If the newly-lit lamp is covered over, even lovers will stumble in the dark. Some couples must be afraid that the power will run out, because they only bring out their marriage-lamp at Christmas or anniversary or when the in-laws are around. The rest of the year they throw cold water on each other.

Another interesting thing about love: it makes light not only for the partner, but for everyone else! Have you gone into a home where love really was, and felt warmth seeping out of the corners?

In the same way your light must shine before people, so that they will see the good things you do and praise your Father in heaven.

Jesus says that love is not only a personal matter, it becomes a public event! He says that people really notice and are deeply touched when love is present. Lives are changed. Happiness and comfort abound!

__________ and __________, you've invited us here today to show us about love. By your vows and agreements, you're telling us that there is light in your lives. You have been the agent of warmth to each other. You have brought out hope, courage and strength in them. You have cracked the dimness of their aloneness with the specialness which only you can bring. And now, you're sharing that with us!

Contagious, isn't it?

We, in turn, are responding by remembering where we last put our own lamps. Some of us will happily readjust the wick and proudly polish the stand. Others will rush home, blow off the dust and anxiously sweat out the time until the spark once again kindles the ashy wick.

__________ and __________, some days you'll have to guard the flame of your lamps against the weather. Winds of temper and rains of despair may threaten your fire. But as you continue to recall what you've expressed here — as you continue to remember your loves and your dreams — you will indeed spread the light of love within your home and that of your neighbor.

May your love light up the corners of your house!

May that light spill forth from your doors and windows to welcome the traveler!

And may God richly bless your marriage, and grant you peace.

Ask, and it will be given you; seek, and you will find; knock, and it will be opened to you. For every one who asks receives, and he who seeks finds, and to him who knocks it will be opened.

(Matthew 7:7-8)

Matthew 7:7-8 | *Not Satisfied With Less*

Once upon a time, in a far-off land, there lived a wise and popular king. He lived in quiet splendor, surrounded by the respect and loyalty of his subjects. The king had three sons, all handsome lads — but alas, they were blind.

As the sons grew into adolescence, the king would often remind them, "Since you cannot see, you must rely upon your other senses to tell you what the world is like." And so one day he sent them off with the Grand Vizier to "see" an elephant. Upon their return, the father asked each son what the elephant was like.

The first son, who had stood by the animal's side, reported, "The elephant is large and smooth; it is like a large piece of marble."

The second son, who had approached the elephant's leg, disagreed: "No, the elephant is round and tall; it is like a tree."

But the third son, who had grasped the beast's tail, retorted, "You are both wrong! The elephant is long and flexible; it is like a rope!"

And the king explained to his observant sons that each had experienced a part of the elephant correctly, but that there was more to the total picture.

That seems to be a constant message of Jesus about the Kingdom of God. We can experience parts very thoroughly, but if we settle for only part, our experience is incomplete. He often points out that we forget to seek out the wholeness of the Kingdom, although this is directly available.

> *Ask, and you will receive; seek, and you will find; knock, and the door will be opened. For everyone who asks receives, he who seeks finds, and to him who knocks, the door will be opened.*

This section of the Sermon on the Mount encourages us to look for the best, to trust in God for rich blessings — and then to expect them as facts already accomplished!

Good things come to the one who asks.

__________ and __________, your marriage is something like that. You can, I suppose, be like the blind sons of the wise king: you can explore your marriage by bits and pieces, but unless you're willing to examine the whole picture, and compare notes on the way, you'll be overwhelmed and confused by substantial differences.

But, if you take seriously the Word of the Lord, you can receive rich gifts and be able to perceive the complete picture! Jesus, of course, is referring to our relationship with God: ask, seek, knock. He means that we shouldn't be afraid or aloof from God, for he wishes to open the heavenly door.

Yet I believe that Jesus also was setting a model for our lives with each other, as well:

- If you will ask, with faith in each other —
- If you will seek, knowing that the other can be found —
- If you will knock, assured that even doors of silence and anxiety are bursting to be opened —

then you will find that your Life Together is full of joy and mutual respect!

__________ and __________, you know full well that this experience of marriage is something you'll have to work at. There will be days when it will seem like an elephant: impossible to move around, costing too much to feed . . . Maybe you'll be tempted to pack your trunk!

But be aware, in times both good and bad, that the wholeness of your Life depends upon the wholeness of your relationship to God. Don't be timid of God or each other. Ask. Seek. Knock.

> For everyone who asks receives, he who seeks finds, and to him who knocks, the door will be opened.

Live boldly, then, in your love — and God will bless you in all goodness.

In the beginning was the Word, and the Word was with God, and the Word was God. In him was life, and the life was the light of men.

(John 1:1, 4)

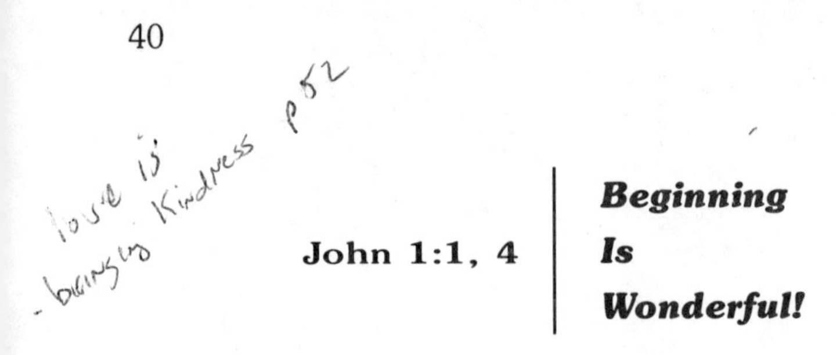

John 1:1, 4

Beginning Is Wonderful!

One of the common songs sung or played at marriages is the Carpenters' "We've Only Just Begun." It's a song about beginnings, which is what weddings are about. About white lace and promises. It's about the joyful anticipation of the road that lies ahead.

Weddings are indeed a celebration of beginnings.

Everything had to start somewhere. What triggered this magical moment? What were the catalysts which brought together the right chemical reaction? How did it all begin?

God reminds us in his Word that beginnings are important. He tells us that we are part of a growth process, that nothing is static, that it is his will and intent that an orderly movement is desirable and Godlike. The beginning, or prologue, of the Good News according to Saint John starts this way:

When all things began, the Word already was.

In a few syllables, we're to know that in the thunderous opening of the Creation, God was there — and *in charge*! The Bible reminds us in all of its parts that whatever begins begins under the tutelage and care of God. We have an assurance that his order prevails, and that there is a divine logic in the flow of life and our history-events.

John also says, "All that came to be was alive with his life, and that life was the light of men." Our beginnings are not cold and powerless markings of an overturned hourglass — but they are vital and surging with an inner drive.

Our message to you this day must be that this a
beginning can signify the loving interest God shares with His People. In other words, his already-created Word is *life*!

__________ and __________, this is truly Good News for your wedding! As you stand here with your friends and family, you have the exciting privilege to begin your formal lives together! I want you to know that God cares about each of you, and that he cares about the marriage which this ceremony introduces. You have the comfort of realizing that the God of Order and Direction has provided for the significant beginnings which we undergo. It is he who began us, and not we ourselves.

Not only did God provide for the beginning of your life together, he has filled it with aliveness and verve, in order that you may be glad in each other and in the joys of each day.

__________ and __________, you also must know that your marriage will consist of more than today's beginning. There will be those occasional tomorrows when upsets creep in, when anger and perhaps a little stubbornness rear their heads and hiss. You know this, of course, since each of you is a true individual with special gifts and values of your own. Yet even in the midst of crises, God is still in charge and is interested in you. He doesn't love you and leave you; nor will his church. As your marriage develops, let God *be* God — and let him take charge of your life, from beginning to end!

Ah, yes — the End.

God has made provision for the totality of your days. Live these days each in the promise and covenant that you are making today — and they will be filled with peace and hopefulness.

You are helping us to relive the beginnings we each have made, and thus to review our own lives in God's grace. Live and love for us, and before us. Help us to see the Divine in your Beginnings. And though you've only just begun, please know that we offer you our sincere support as you anticipate the road that lies ahead.

These things I have spoken to you, that my joy may be in you, and that your joy may be full.

"This is my commandment, that you love one another as I have loved you. Greater love has no man than this, that a man lay down his life for his friends. You are my friends if you do what I command you. No longer do I call you servants, for the servant does not know what his master is doing; but I have called you friends, for all that I have heard from my Father I have made known to you. You did not choose me, but I chose you and appointed you that you should go and bear fruit and that your fruit should abide; so that whatever you ask the Father in my name, he may give it to you. This I command you, to love one another.

(John 15:11-17)

John 15:11-17

No Greater Love

In Charles Dickens' *A Tale of Two Cities*, Joseph Carton traded places with a condemned man going to the guillotine in the French Revolution. "'Tis a far, far better thing I do," said he, "than any other thing . . ." And we know of other touching stories, some of them quite real, about a noble person volunteering their own life in order that others may live.

Nathan Hale.

The Unknown Soldier.

Benigno Aquino.

Jesus Christ.

This is my commandment: love one another, as I have loved you. There is no greater love than this, that a man should lay down his life for his friends.

A strange text for a wedding-day!

There've been *enough* bad jokes already about marriage as slavery and death! Yet the very newness of the marriage ceremony speaks of abandoning some of the old in order to taste some of the new. And that's where we need to be careful of the analogy. For some of the old has been very good, and worth keeping!

No bride (or groom either, for that matter) wants to alter their partner; for that would destroy the whole personality, the entire loveableness, of their spouse. Lou Costello has defined a husband as "what's left of a sweetheart after the nerve has been killed."

"Love one another, as I have loved you," Jesus said. The

"laying down" of life is an exercise in exchanging our daily comings and goings for an eternal commitment.

Listen again to the words of the vows — words like "sickness" and "health," like "richer" and "poorer." "Until we are parted by death" is a radical statement!

__________ and __________, you've come here today to make those words public. It should surprise no one that these vows can be connected with Joy. "I have spoken thus to you, so that my joy may be in you, and your joy complete." We sometimes get so wrapped up in the correctness and procedure of marriage that we forget the Joy!

Wedding families may leave out the Joy because they're thinking ahead to paying for the reception!

Disgruntled friends and lovers may be unjoyful because they're trapped in what might have been.

And some wedding guests haven't wanted to come at all, so they look as though they had nails for lunch . . .

Still, God calls us to a Joy —

Easter is accomplished;
we have hope in Christ;
and two of God's People are getting married!

__________ and __________, don't let anyone steal your Joy! There will be days, no doubt, when each of you may want to nurse the grudge a little more — to irritate a wound until it becomes infected — to poke at the scars of times past.

Don't do it.

There's no virtue in that kind of suffering.

An old clergyman was once marrying a couple. And because he was very nearsighted, he moved close to them. He moved so close that he stepped — hard — on the bride's toe. She spoke not a word, although he was a heavy man. Finally aware of his blunder, he asked, "My dear, why didn't you tell me I was hurting you?" In pain, the bride sobbed, "I thought it was part of the ceremony!"

Pain has no part of our ceremony — or our marriage. But *joy* does, a heavenly joy of completeness and giving.

Receive God's joy: of belonging, of giving away, of sharing the treasure.

> *This is my commandment: love one another, as I have loved you. There is no greater love than this, but a man should lay down his life for his friends.*

For I am sure that neither death, nor life, nor angels, nor principalities, nor things present, nor things to come, nor powers, nor height, nor depth, nor anything else in all creation, will be able to separate us from the love of God in Christ Jesus our Lord.

(Romans 8:38-39)

Romans 8:38-39

No Strings Cut

"Family Ties" is a weekly TV drama which started as a foolish sit-com, but gained character. During the life of the show, we've watched the smart-aleck teen-aged son, Alex, grow from being a token jerk into a complex young man. Alex dreams, but not all of his dreams work the way he expects. Alex talks like a big shot, but turns out to be pleasantly vulnerable. Alex is just like us.

Where "Family Ties" is *not* like us, of course, is in the fact that our own complexities of life don't generally become resolved in a half-hour! Still and all, the show does generate a closeness by program's end, despite the different lifestyles of Alex and his family.

God has a great program of Family Ties, too! From the very beginning, when he created men and women and provided for children. God had this idea about being close and responsible. As we've been created in his Image, we can see God himself as a being of intimacy. Jesus told us that we're not to hold him at arm's length, but that we can call him "Daddy." Our God is a God of closeness, of embracing, or reconciliation.

Our God blesses our marriages, removes them from the everydayness of social custom by announcing that the Kingdom of Heaven much resembles a wedding feast, and that the church shall be and already is the Bride of Christ! Our God is a God of visible love.

Christians at Rome in the early days were considered subversives, and their worship was outlawed. If they visibly expressed God's love, they literally put their lives on the line. Saint Paul said this to them:

For I am certain that nothing can separate us from his love: neither death nor life, neither angels nor other heavenly rulers or powers, neither the present nor the future, neither the world above nor the world below — there is nothing in all creation that will ever be able to separate us from the love of God which is ours through Jesus Christ our Lord.

These are powerful words, thundering with hope through times of brokenness and insecurity.

These are gentle words, allowing us to find serenity even though all around us are breaking apart.

These are words appropriate to a marriage, reminding us that there is nothing which can successfully stand between God and his people!

I give them to you, __________ and __________, so that you can know and affirm that God's Love *does* triumph over all earthly problems.

The two of you have come here today to affirm your love before your family and friends. You've come also to affirm your faith in the God of Love who rejoices with you. You've come to formalize a covenant of respect and responsibility which you have privately pledged but now publicly own.

__________ and __________, you're well aware of the pitfalls which can ensnare your relationship. You know the apprehensions which can come with a newness of partners and places. There will be days in which you may well need to be reminded that love is a divine quality. There will be days when the bacon is burned.

But through good times and bad, you can hear the echo of God's Love, a love which no traditions or authorities or disillusionments can overcome.

There is nothing in all creation that will ever be able to separate us from the love of God which is ours *through Christ Jesus our Lord.*

As we were planning this ceremony, I expressed concern

that I wouldn't be able to get the rings from the pillow. "Shall I keep a small pair of scissors handy?" I asked. And you replied, __________, "No; there'll be no strings cut!" So this is a fine slogan for the establishment of our own Family Ties.

Some will see it as a sitcom, and laugh and cry with us.

Others may analyze it for social content, and may overlook the joy.

But one thing's for certain: It'll last for more than half-an-hour!

Let love be genuine; hate what is evil, hold fast to what is good.

(Romans 12:9)

Romans 12:9 | ***The Nobility of Love***

Cinderella turned sadly away from the Photo-Quik booth, and sighed in despair, "*Some*day my prints will come . . ."

Cinderella's plight is a common one. The analyst C. G. Jung called the Cinderella tale perfect, since it contained the basic descriptions of our lives:

- Being misunderstood.
- Being stuck in a corner where our natural beauty and talents aren't discovered.
- Having to humble our own purity in the face of arrogance.
- And finally — miracle of miracles — getting to the ball despite all odds, and being discovered by the one who will make your life complete!

Some folks prefer to take more initiative. A more recent Cinderella had been known to remark, "You have to kiss a lot of frogs before one will turn into a prince!" We're reminded of the cartoon in *Mad* magazine where the beautiful princess kissed a frog — and immediately turned *herself* into a frog! Water seeks its own level . . .

Thomas Oden, in his book *Game Free: the Meaning of Intimacy,* has a delightful chapter entitled "A Letter to Frogs and Princes." Actually it's his paraphrase of Saint Paul's letter to the Christians at Rome, some of which we've just heard. But the letter to Romans and frogs and princes is a letter of encouragement, Oden says. The point is, you don't have to be tied up in game transactions, bound up in traditional scripts not of your own choosing. We can, says Saint Paul, be set free from the Law of Sin and Death which ties us up in knots of guilt and stunts our growth. Our model, of course, is not a fairy godmother, but

Jesus Christ, who comes bursting into our daily swamps with a message of love and potential of life! A passage from Romans which springs out at me today says, "Love in all sincerity, loathing evil and clinging to the good."

__________ and __________, this seems very fitting for your wedding and for the richness of life which will proceed from this day on. If you love in sincerity, you'll never be bothered with halfway measures. You'll not have self-doubts, nor will you be plagued by loneliness. (Not all that masquerades as love really *is* — and there are those who suffer from insincerity.) But if you truly put aside any games with each other, if you truly decide that intimacy is a complete merging of one being with another, then your love will be sincere.

Paul continues, "loathe evil, cling to the good."

What good advice for the newly intimate!

Don't even listen to any junky stuff — about yourself, about the other, about *anybody*.

Take yourselves at face value.

Believe in each other.

Cling to the good.

__________ and __________, every marriage needs a lot of clinging. I hope that you'll always physically cling to each other, touching and reassuring each other until you're at least a hundred and four. Don't strangle each other: just *support* each other.

But especially, *cling* — to the good stuff.

When one or the other is late, remember all the times he or she was early!

When one or the other forgets an important event, remember all the times he or she *did* remember!

And when your own bad days occur and the waters of anxiety get high, cling to the stable points in your marriage, remembering that love is real and that you've shared so much already.

Our Christian faith and our own experience assures us that love is noble. All who love become princes and princesses in their own right. In God's grace, we can hop to our freedom to love, knowing that God *is* love.

Love in all sincerity, loathing evil and clinging to the good.

For the foolishness of God is wiser than men, and the weakness of God is stronger than men.

(1 Corinthians 1:25)

1 Corinthians 1:25 | ***Stronger Than Strong***

This is an age of outrageous advertising.

The makers of old-time Oxydol created a stampede when they advertised that their laundry detergent could "beat the sun." Now everyone and their brother makes humongous claims about their product:

"Lasts forever!"

"Tastes great, less filling!"

"Stronger than strong!"

The problem is that few of these claims have any merit whatsoever! We've gotten so inured to this flood of overstatement that we really don't *expect* things to work or taste or deliver as their backers have promised. Our reaction to something perhaps legitimately fantastic is a bored, "Yeah, sure."

Unfortunately, this kind of myth has also attached itself to our current expectation of marriage. There was a period, I suppose, when brides and grooms lived in the folklore of German hero-legends, which always ended by the happy couple escaping to a far-off land where they lived happily ever after. I'm glad we've outgrown *that* one!

Then there's the "Pygmalion/My Fair Lady" myth, which says that one partner can reform/remake the other. This doesn't work, either. Besides, it's not nice to manipulate your spouse to achieve your personal ends.

So our overly-cynical, over-advertised commentary to those contemplating marriage usually turns out to be a herd of poor jokes:

"Why should you do that?" or

"Now you'll be suffering like the rest of us;" or

"Well, your troubles are at an end — but we won't say which end!"

Thus our contemporary folklore proclaims marriage either an evil to be avoided or a condition to be endured!

Saint Paul did write various thoughts about marriage to the Corinthian congregation — but I'm not sure the passage we just heard was specifically for that purpose. Looking at a wider spectrum, the Apostle was trying to point out that Christ was the entirety of God's wisdom and power. And he was affirming that some things which the rest of the world poke fun at are actually the things that last and prove meaningful!

> *For what seems to be God's foolishness is wiser than human wisdom, and what seems to be God's weakness is stronger than human strength.*

__________ and __________, you've come here today to show those who'd scoff that there really *is* something to this marriage bit! The vows that you take and the symbols you exchange are all part of a certainty on your part that you are indeed entering into something holy and right.

You have a lot of courage. It's not easy to stand up in front of God and the whole Village and say that you honestly believe in the sanctity of marriage . . . and in each other.

And so, __________ and __________, I'll clue you in on a little secret. It's this: you can't do it by yourself! If your marriage is to remain holy, you need to look to the *source* of holiness. This God, who created men and women for each other, is the underlying foundation of love, commitment, trust, sacrifice.

Another word for all of this is marriage.

Our own wisdom turns out to be so much dust in the wind. Our own strength fails miserably. Yet the Word of the Lord endures forever.

And so, as you join yourselves to each other, allow God's own power and wisdom to join with you. Stand together in peace and the assurance of God's overriding love. And, may the unsurpassed joy of this day continue within your home and hearts *each* day, now and forever.

God bless you.

Love is patient and kind; love is not jealous or boastful; it is not arrogant or rude. Love does not insist on its own way; it is not irritable or resentful; it does not rejoice at wrong, but rejoices in the right. Love bears all things, believes all things, hopes all things, endures all things.

(1 Corinthians 13:4-7)

1 Corinthians 13:4-7

But Not Frozen In Stone

One of my earliest recollections of our city was as a young man, coming across the Market Street Bridge and seeing the tall and magnificent statue of the crucified Christ atop King's College. Stark against the skyline by day, and lit warmly by night, the statue of Our Lord looks down upon the city: on the trees in the Common, and the fountains on the square; on the dark alleys and shuttered houses as well as the pleasant, well-lighted neighborhoods.

Maybe some of you can remember when the statue went up — but to my mind, it has always been there. And its solidarity implies that it always will be there.

There are other statues in town. Blind justice on the Courthouse. Uncomfortable eagles on the bridge. Free-form sculpture on the Square. Assorted monuments to people and events. They help us to capture not only a heritage, but remind us of a time coming in which they shall be continued in celebration.

Saint Paul speaks about Love in this manner! There's a solidness, a timelessness in these rolling phrases:

> *Love is patient and kind; love is not jealous or boastful; it is not arrogant or rude. Love does not insist on its own way; it is not irritable or resentful; it does not rejoice at wrong, but rejoices in the right. Love bears all things, believes all things, hopes all things, endures all things.*

He wants us to know that love — and lovers — have such attributes. Patience and kindness, hope and endurance: like the statue, these stand in the midst of sunshine and rain, firm and good and waiting.

Love doesn't rush madly about, blowing its own horn, and trying to outdo or push others away!

Love doesn't step right in and say, "See, I *told* you so!"

But love *does* help to pick up the pieces of eroded dreams — and leads the way in cementing them once again into a useable form.

__________ and __________, this long-awaited day is here when you stand with each other — and us — to make a covenant in terms which echo those of Saint Paul. You've pledged to stick with each other with the steadfastness of the statue, and to support each other with all your person, come what may. And you are also indicating that you will not jump on the other one, *even if you are obviously right*! (There will be occasions, I'm certain, when one of you will surely make superior decisions despite the blundering of the other.) And then there will be other times when you'll thank your partner for not being a Know-it-all constantly!

__________ and __________, stand firm like the statue — firm in your love. But don't be so wooden, so stony that you can't unbend a bit —

- when your partner comes with a hurting heart and a six-pack of mistakes;
- when your household tends to become silent from stubborn insistence;
- when other persons' good advice may drive a wedge into a yet reparable rift.

Then, especially, make sure that you take the first step to go to the other in peace.

My good friends, I feel so solid about *you*.

I have a conviction that you're going to hold firm despite any changes in the weather!

So, as you go from here as husband and wife, be to *us* a timeless symbol, lifted up and lighted on our horizon: proclaim love in all its trueness; live with each other fully and honestly; and welcome each day — not as a challenge to survive, but as an opportunity to grow even stronger.

May the love of our Living Lord constantly be with you.

Love is patient and kind; love is not jealous or boastful; it is not arrogant or rude. Love does not insist on its own way; it is not irritable or resentful; it does not rejoice at wrong, but rejoices in the right. Love bears all things, believes all things, hopes all things, endures all things.

(1 Corinthians 13:4-7)

1 Corinthians 13:4-7 | *Keeping No Score*

It would have been better had they all stayed away.

The movie *Butterfly* is a tragedy about love. Our Hero has faithfully watched over the old silver mine ever since his wife and daughters left him, years before. But the story really begins when the youngest daughter returns. Did she come for her father, or use him to get rich from the old mine? And once she showed up, to disrupt the father's moral simplicity, the door seemed to open for all the resurrected ghosts of the past to enter and to prey upon his notions of love.

It's a psychological tragedy, and we don't really know for sure if these people are real — or subconscious mirages which have come from being out in the desert too long.

The worth of the story lies in its dealings with love, and what each one thinks love is.

- Some think that love is a remembrance of poetic and passionate encounters of an earlier life.
- Others think that love is a tool for manipulation of all you can get out of today.
- Still others think that love is a soft cloud that makes one feel good, no matter what happens around them.

Saint Paul defines love admirably to the Christian community at Corinth: Love is patient; love is kind and envies no one. Love is never boastful, nor conceited, nor rude; never selfish, not quick to take offense. Love keeps no score of wrongs; does not gloat over other person's sins, but delights in the truth. There is nothing love cannot face; there is no limit to its faith, its hope, and its endurance.

These attributes, Paul says, make the difference between real and tragic love. And it seems to me that there can be no other choices but those — real or tragic. This is true because love that is not love only leads to destruction, broken dreams and out-takes of would-be scenes on the cutting room floor. Love that is not love breeds distress, and abrogates the once-rehearsed script which was our vision from childhood.

__________ and __________, listen carefully to the words of the Apostle. Your marriage will need all the patience and kindness you can give it. You will need to learn not to keep score, for obligation can ruin a marriage just as duty can wreck a profession.

But most important of all, concentrate on Paul's promise: "There is nothing love cannot face . . ." If this can be the sticking-point for your life together, there will be no limit to your endurance — and you'll be able to hang together despite separations, codicils and briefs, blueprints and specifications, parents and co-workers!

__________ and __________, we've all come today to stand with you as you make covenant with each other. More than curious observers, each of us has a special interest in your joining together. We're here to be your friends, to offer you our support in making it work. And in many small ways, we're here also to ratify the covenants in our own lives which may have accumulated the prosaic dust of self-interest.

The butterfly is one of God's beautiful creatures, a symbol of his Love and resurrection. What once was apparently dead has again broken into life, with an unexpected radiance and the ability to move in a whole new dimension.

Yet some varieties of these noble images can be destructive, can defoliate the forests of your hopes until only barren rock remains.

Look for the real.

Be patient and kind.

And, keep no score of wrongs. Instead, believe that love can face anything. And surely, there will be no limits to your endurance, and your life together will be blessed.

For you were called to freedom, brethren; only do not use your freedom as an opportunity for the flesh, but through love be servants of one another. For the whole law is fulfilled in one word, "You shall love your neighbor as yourself. But if you bite and devour one another take heed that you are not consumed by one another.

(Galatians 5:13-15)

Galatians 5:13-15 | *Love at First Sight*

Love is always blind, they say. And it's a good thing, especially in the case of Roy and Shirley. These characters, in the movie *Love at First Sight,* are blind to a certain degree. He really can't see. And she's decided to overlook all the kinky parts of his erratic nature.

The movie goes on to explain that these two had been the girl and boy next door, always a nice American romantic setting for a marriage. (Today, on the other hand, most of us think that happens *only* in the movies!) But Roy and Shirley had indeed known each other earlier, and thus their romance reclaimed a lifetime of good experiences.

I doubt that it ever really is "love at first sight." I think that Love is a gradual process which sparks and develops between two persons as they share in many things together. We're reminded here of the old cannibal joke, where the chief asks his daughter if she enjoyed their dinner guest on the previous evening: "Oh yes, Dad," she replied. "It was love at first *bite*!"

The Apostle Paul has much to say about our personal relationships, especially as we've been touched by the love of Jesus Christ. He writes to the Christians at Galatia, which is part of the modern country of Turkey —

> *For you were called to freedom, brethren; only do not use your freedom as an opportunity for the flesh, but through love be servants of one another. For the whole law is fulfilled in one word, "You shall love your neighbor as yourself." But if you bite and devour one another, take heed that you are not consumed by one another.*

This has to do with marriage, as well as anything else. The "opportunity for the flesh" Paul decries is that idea some people nurture that the momentary should take precedence over the long-term commitment. As we love our neighbor — next-door or otherwise — we are tying ourselves into a long-range understanding that we live for each other, that what we are and what we become is important to others. But if we eat each other up there will be, like the snake that ate its tail, nothing left of us either.

__________ and __________, this is the day for your neighborhood to rejoice. It says something good about all of the neighborhood when two of its offspring decide to join together in commitments and love. We can see that there have been good things happening during your formative years. Each one of us can stick out our chests a bit!

There will be times, I suppose, when things don't seem so good, when you'll want to say to each other, "You always *were* a spoiled brat!" There will be times when childhood annoyances and youthful impunities come back to haunt you. But having gone through all that already, you can look back and laugh — and the anger will soon pass.

__________ and __________, you have much going for you as the boy and girl next door. You know each other's foibles and families, the relatives and the reservations. You've gone past the Love-at-first-Sight — or "Bite" — stage. You are here to affirm your life together, and we are ready to affirm you as a new family.

Go in peace, together, eating of the fruit of God's Holy Spirit — love, joy, patience, kindness, gentleness, self-control.

And whether or not Love is Blind, see deeply into each other.

See All.

Love All.

May it ever be.

"For this reason a man shall leave his father and mother and be joined to his wife, and the two shall become one flesh."

This mystery is a profound one, and I am saying that it refers to Christ and the church; however, let each one of you love his wife as himself, and let the wife see that she respects her husband.

(Ephesians 5:31-33)

Ephesians 5:31-33 | *Getting No Respect?*

Rodney Dangerfield is a person to whom we all relate.

Rodney is a character, not a real person. He typifies everyone, in some way. Oily-haired, bug-eyed Rodney is always trying to fit in — like a sore thumb, or an extra wheel. He tries too hard. He's misunderstood. He ends up the goat.

Rodney "don't get no respect." He makes us feel good: he carries our foibles and frustrations to an extreme. We laugh with him, not at him, realizing that he may well be an important side of us!

Much of our world turns without proper love or respect. Although we ourselves have tender spots, we tend to hide them as best as possible and go our way. Insensitive to others, we momentarily are able to forget our own sensitivity. Most of the world goes through the motions without getting too deeply involved, without digging down to where the realities of soul and personality lie. The Christian Church maintains that marriage shouldn't be such a surface exercise, but that each of the partners must become imbedded in each other. To do so, we become vulnerable.

If we love each other enough to show our Achilles' heel, enough to uncover the soft spots, we risk. We know that our partner can either use these spots as targets to destroy us, or that they will treat us tenderly, respecting our frailties and loving us more.

Saint Paul writes to us through the congregation at Ephesus,

As the Scripture says, "For this reason a man will leave his father and mother and unite with his wife, and the two will become one." There is a deep secret truth revealed in this Scripture, which I understand as applying to Christ and the church. But it also applies to you: every husband must love his wife as himself, and every wife must respect her husband.

When "two become as one" there is a merger of business, a sharing of concerns. When two become as one, even illness or other difficulty becomes a family matter. Christ and the church, Paul says, are so united in spiritual richness, in the mutuality of goals, plans and hopes.

Thus in our Christian marriages we see that love and respect melt the separations.

__________ and __________, you've come here this day to make public your desires of becoming vulnerable and sensitive to each other. It's a step and an occasion not to be taken lightly. This service calls each of us who witness it to examine our own sensitivities once again. You are coming to dare the respect and love which marriage demands.

There will be days, __________ and __________, when you may feel tempted to poke about in the vulnerable spots of your partner. There will be days on which you would prefer to draw the curtains of your life tightly about you, neither giving nor taking.

This is not unusual.

But recall, especially on those days, the wisdom of the Apostle:

Every husband must love his wife as himself, and every wife must respect her husband.

As you leave here, be joined as one —

- in your vulnerabilities and your dreams;
- in your foibles and your inspirations;
- in your mistakes and in your glories . . .

And don't let your partner say (unless they're joking) "I don't get no respect."

Rejoice in the Lord always; again I will say, Rejoice. Let all men know your forbearance, The Lord is at hand. Have no anxiety about anything, but in everything by prayer and supplication with thanksgiving let your requests be made known to God. And the peace of God, which passes all understanding, will keep your hearts and your minds in Christ Jesus.

Finally, brethren, whatever is true, whatever is honorable, whatever is just, whatever is pure, whatever is lovely, whatever is gracious, if there is any excellence, if there is anything worthy of praise, think about these things. What you have learned and received and heard and seen in me, do; and the God of peace will be with you.

(Philippians 4:4-9)

Philippians 4:4-9 | *Love Is Lovelier . . .*

It's probably corny to even bring it up, but Frank Sinatra's song surely runs through our minds today!

The idea of reclaiming lost love is a noble and fascinating one. Most of us secretly wish for a chance to try again with our first true love; and here, right before your eyes, folks, it's happening!

Maybe what makes "the second time around" lovelier is the mellowing of life during the intervening years. As we move along the paths of our journey, our values become clearer. We define our expectations more completely, and have learned to demand less quantity in favor of the moments of quality.

The Apostle Paul has some words for us about defining our expectations. As he was, we are waiting for the fulfillment of the covenant, waiting for the coming of Christ in glory. The Apostle has given the Philippians some words of cheer to define their waiting: He speaks of being joyful in union with the Lord; of having a gentle attitude and a thankful heart. He tells them — and us — to *fill* the mind with the stuff of endurance: "things that are true, noble, right, pure, lovely, and honorable." As Christians wait on the brink of fulfillment, these words give credibility to our waiting, and a reason to look confidently at the future.

__________ and __________, you stand here before us with both feet on the ground. For you this is a time of expectation. With you we dare affirm that something is going to happen. You are rightly pointing out to God's people gathered here that there *is* an advantage to waiting with expectation. You are proclaiming that it's never too late!

__________ and __________, there may well be days when you candidly wonder if love will *ever* arrive. Lonely and cold days. Heartless days of not caring. But you've been there before, and now you have a sure hope of love which is becoming clearer! Learning from the past paves the road of the future!

At any rate, here you are, dressed again in the clothes of expectation, ready and willing once again to recreate a new covenant. There's something Holy in all of this. It's as if God is saying, "Despite the broken promises and tarnished dreams of yesterday, a new love can be loved."

A New Life is on our doorstep. Promises are being made again. Love is lovelier, the second time around.

Put on then, as God's chosen ones, holy and beloved, compassion, kindness, lowliness, meekness, and patience, forbearing one another and, if one has a complaint against another, forgiving each other; as the Lord has forgiven you, so you also must forgive. And above all these put on love, which binds everything together in perfect harmony.

(Colossians 3:12-14)

Colossians 3:12-14

The Crowning Virtue

There's something real and lasting about arches.

An arch is a structure that builders use when they wish to distribute the weight of a building or bridge equally between two pillars, without putting undue stress on either.

Arches are celebrated in the spans of ancient Roman aqueducts and the flying buttresses of medieval cathedrals.

Arches join our skyline in the free-flowing sculpture which greets visitors to Saint Louis and in the ever-present Golden Arches which welcome hungry travelers to Ronald McDonald land.

God created the arch when he made the Egg, and commemorated it in the Rainbow.

Saint Paul, one of the arch-itects of the expression of Christianity, makes some allusions to this construction. "To crown all," he says, "there must be love, to bind all together and complete the whole."

We're tempted to think of "crown" as the ornate jewelry given to monarchs for the symbolization of their realm. (And that's an all-right metaphor, especially on such a royal occasion as a wedding!) But I think Saint Paul is talking about arches: after the columns are built, straight and tall; after they've begun to lean over toward each other; then the crown, the keystone, is placed between them, to absorb and direct the pressures from above, to distribute the burdens and the stress . . . This love does indeed bind all together. It completes the whole.

__________ and __________, this occasion publicly confirms the arching together of your lives. You've grown individually, strengthened and formed by the care of your families and friends.

And now you've leaned together, and we celebrate yo
ing. This celebration is the capstone, the crown of your love.

__________ and __________, the Apostle has more good words for your marriage —

> *Then put on the garments that suit God's chosen people, his own, his beloved: compassion, kindness, humility, gentleness, patience. Be forbearing with one another, and forgiving, where any of you has cause for complaint: you must forgive as the Lord forgave you.*

He's saying, in effect, that since God entered into a covenant with his people, that you also should enter such a covenant. The covenant you make this day reflects God's marriage with his bride, the church. We're to adopt certain virtues —

- Compassion and kindness are necessary for your lives together, since you are taking each other as part of your own bodies. (Will you help each other when the dark hours of the spirit roll by?)
- Humility and gentleness can heal when angry words fly and when "I told you so" seems a bitter triumph within a mutual defeat.
- And patience, of course. Patience which will quietly wait when purses are forgotten or car keys misplaced, patience which will calmly persevere when household tasks have slipped into another tomorrow . . .
- But the crowning virtue is Love. Love combines the cosmic forces into one person, love which allows subjection and obedience without harshness. This love continues to grow. It will solidify your home, and if children come to you, it will increase your strength as a family unit.

Remember the arches. When properly crowned, they distribute the weight. If your lives are joined together and crowned with love, you'll be able to withstand the weighty matters of today's families.

Don't stand around with fallen arches! The God who loves you and who gives you his Word will always be ready to keep the crown of love on the arch of your marriage!

Wives, be subject to your husbands, as is fitting in the Lord. Husbands, love your wives, and do not be harsh with them. Children, obey your parents in everything, for this pleases the Lord. Fathers, do not provoke your children, lest they become discouraged. Slaves, obey in everything those who are your earthly masters, not with eyeservice, as men-pleasers, but in singleness of heart, fearing the Lord. Whatever your task, work heartily, as serving the Lord, and not men, knowing that from the Lord you will receive the inheritance as your reward; you are serving the Lord Christ. For the wrongdoer will be paid back for the wrong he has done, and there is no partiality.

Masters, treat your slaves justly and fairly, knowing that you also have a Master in heaven.

(Colossians 3:18—4:1)

Colossians 3:18—4:1 | ***House Calls***

Dr. Charley Nichols enjoyed jogging, and really worked at it. During the day, he was an off-the-wall medic at a Los Angeles hospital. At night he enjoyed playing games. Charley's whole life was a game — a game that gave him a decreasing amount of satisfaction until he met Ann.

Ann Atkinson had been married, just like Charley. But the script hadn't come out right, and she saw most of her dreams and plans lying like so many scraps on the cutting-room floor of her life. The movie "House Calls" is Neil Simon's commentary on the games we play with ourselves and the people we love, while we're trying to identify the mysteries of this time and place.

God knows that life can be serious enough, that we need to make a game out of some things. But God also knows that personal relationships are not for playing around, but that they become a vital part of what we are and who we are.

The Scriptures are full of God's Word concerning personal relationships: The Ten Commandments; Amos; the Song of Solomon. The Gospel is the dramatization of God's reconciliation within relationships. And Saint Paul has written words we just read about Christian domestic ethics.

> *Be subject to your husbands . . . Love your wives . . . obey your parents . . . give obedience.*

And then he says,

> *Whatever you are doing, put your whole heart into it, as if you were doing it for the Lord and not for men, knowing that there is a Master who will give you your heritage as a reward for your service.*

That's where we need especially to touch down today. __________ and __________, in your marriage, "whatever you are doing, put your whole heart into it . . ."

It seems clear that the success of your life together hinges upon putting your whole heart into your marriage. In the case of *big*, of course, you know the worth of deciding together about home and children, of major purchases and household policy. But put your whole heart into even the *little*, the *trivial* things — such as who signs the Christmas cards, what time supper should be served, which chair is "my" chair, and who's going to turn out the lights.

Whatever you're doing, put all you've got into it, just as if you were doing it for God.

Really, you *are* doing it for God. He cares mightily for you as individuals and as a valid couple. Not only does he care for you, but he's willing and able to stand with you to help you through the spots that are richer or poorer, better or worse.

__________ and __________, there'll be times of joy and anxiety in your life together. Some days everything will fall into place smoothly. But other days you'll feel as though you're stuck in a big traffic jam on a beltline interstate a long way from home! Knowing that days will be good or bad is half the battle. And the other half is having the courage, the willpower to stick it out, and *make* it work.

By God, and by his Holy Spirit and his Son Jesus, it will. You've come here to place a godly content on your vows and covenant. As you go from here, understand that that godly presence will continue to enrich your marriage, if you will let it.

We who affirm God's presence in our own relationships know that he "makes house calls" — but he's not playing around.

Love with your whole heart.

Stick by each other.

Go in peace.

Be patient, therefore, brethren, until the coming of the Lord. Behold, the farmer waits for the precious fruit of the earth, being patient over it until it receives the early and the late rain. You also be patient. Establish your hearts, for the coming of the Lord is at hand. Do not grumble, brethren, against one another, that you may not be judged; behold, the Judge is standing at the doors. As an example of suffering and patience, brethren, take the prophets who spoke in the name of the Lord. Behold, we call those happy who were steadfast. You have heard of the steadfastness of Job, and you have seen the purpose of the Lord, how the Lord is compassionate and merciful.

(James 5:7-11)

James 5:7-11 | *Hanging In*

There's an old maxim that I learned at my mother's knee (or some other joint) that goes like this:

> *Patience is a virtue: learn it while you can;*
> *it's seldom known in women, but often found in man.*

Or was it the other way around?

However it's supposed to go, we recognize patience — or the lack of it — in our lives.

Much of our lives are lived in nervous desperation, waiting for the right time, the appointed place.

"Are we there yet?" is the kids' constant chant soon after we leave the driveway.

"What time is it *now*?" asks the expectant father in the obstetric waiting room.

"What time is it *now*?" asks the same man's grandmother, confined to her chair in a long room filled with other aged folk.

And I saw a bumper sticker that read, "Are We Having a Good Time Yet?"

Saint James addressed the problem in his letter to the church. He sensed that many were beginning to think that Jesus would *never* come back — which explained why they were beginning to fall away from faith and to beat up on their brothers and sisters.

He wrote, "See how patient a farmer is as he waits for his land to produce precious crops." The farmer knows that you can't hurry things along. All you can do is to prepare the soil, select the best seed, and cultivate it a bit. After that, Nature must take its course. And at first, it doesn't look like much.

Some will scoff, "You'll never get anything out of *that*!" But by-and-by, a valuable crop comes pushing through!

Now James, of course, is using the analogy to paint a picture of patience for those who wait for the fulfilment of God's Kingdom. But I don't think that it will do violence to the writer's talent to speak about *part* of God's movement here. Let's think especially about Marriage. Patience is certainly a virtue of Marriage! Not only do we do some *physical* waiting for our spouse's agendas to connect with ours, but we do some *spiritual* waiting, as well! I mean that we can't cram all our plans and ideas and hopes down our spouse's throat, but we must *wait* for them to come around . . .

__________ and __________, you've come today to make promises to one another in a public style. And patience is one of those things which underlies your promises. You realize, I'm sure, that you're just like the farmer we read about:

- you've selected what you'll plant in the field of your marriage;
- you've tried to find the rocks and dig them out;
- you've cut the weeds of yesterday and disposed of their debris.

All you can do now is wait.

In seminary, during a time of crisis, we students had buttons printed which said, "To the End." We meant to hang on, to endure until better times. We knew that the Lord provides, in his good time. And so he has. And so he will for you also, as you begin your life together in patience.

__________ and __________, there will always be some who will scoff. Some will try to get you to abandon your hopes and plans and dreams. Yet with the patience which God commends and supplies, the garden of your marriage will flourish and produce.

Two men decided they would go bear hunting. And so, armed and with full gear, they laboriously climbed the mountain. Near the top, the trail forked; and they found a sign which read, “Bear Left.” Disappointed, they went home.

Learn how to read the signs.

Don’t go home disappointed.

And may the Lord, who is “full of mercy and compassion,” add to your love daily.

God bless you.

Are you greater than our father Jacob, who gave us the well, and drank from it himself, and his sons, and his cattle?

(1 John 4:12)

1 John 4:12 | *Seeing the Love*

It's pretty hard to know what Love is. We use the word very carelessly:

- to tell how we feel about Rocky Road ice cream;
- to describe our delight at a lingering sunset;
- or even, in a more sensitive moment, to tell our partner just what it is about them we most like . . .

The poets have tried to capture love in the sound of words —

Perhaps love is like an ocean, ever moving, never still . . .

Some say love is hanging on; others, letting go . . .

Musicians have set love to music, and then realized that the music has generated the sense of love. Albert Einstein was asked to explain the theory of relativity in forty-eight words. "I can't," said Einstein, "but if you'll loan me a violin, I'll *play* it for you in forty-eight *measures*!"

It's pretty hard to know what love is.

Saint John, the beloved Apostle, knew what love is. He spent his ministry preaching and living love — and when he was a very old man, his message to the church was still: "Love one another." He said that love was more than just a nice warm thing for us to do and be. I'm sure that he was aware that those who love and are beings of love usually get love strokes back.

Yet John's message was more than the momentary joys of loving: He said that we could see *God*!

Though God has never been seen by any man, God himself dwells in us if we love one another; his love is brought to perfection within us.

If we want to know what God is like, says the Apostle, we need to love. And, conversely, those who love — purely, giving everything, without manipulation — shall be the dwelling of God!

And, if God himself resides within us, love is brought to perfection.

__________ and __________, on this day as we celebrate your love for one another, we truly desire that your love will be made perfect.

Saint John goes on to say in his letter that "perfect love banishes fear." As your love is whole before God, you needn't fear the judgment of each other, or your family, or your friends.

As your love is whole before God, you don't have to be afraid that you yourself are less-than-worthy. You can be yourselves in front of each other! You can share the laughs of your days at work — and sometimes the disappointments. You can be proud of each other's accomplishments: the lawn well-mowed, the bedroom well-painted, the surprising rose that grew where you had planted sunflowers . . . You can accept each other's funny habits, their grass-stained jeans, their disgusting noises in the morning . . .

__________ and __________, there are some risks. There may well be days when you have to work a bit at perfecting love. There will be days when you have to turn away from your partner's momentary anger, and days when you have to tell them you didn't hear what they said and that you know that they didn't mean it. Even when it hurt a lot.

Live freely and perfectly and without fear together.

Trust in God.

And remember that you have many friends who believe in you and your love.

Then I saw a new heaven and a new earth; for the first heaven and the first earth had passed away, and the sea was no more. And I saw the holy city, new Jerusalem, coming down out of heaven from God, prepared as a bride adorned for her husband; and I heard a loud voice from the throne saying, "Behold, the dwelling of God is with men. He will dwell with them, and they shall be his people, and God himself will be with them; he will wipe away every tear from their eyes, and death shall be no more, neither shall there be mourning nor crying nor pain any more, for the former things have passed away."

And he who sat upon the throne said, "Behold, I make all things new." Also he said, "Write this, for these words are trustworthy and true." And he said to me, "It is done! I am the Alpha and the Omega, the beginning and the end. To the thirsty I will give from the fountain of the water of life without payment. He who conquers shall have this heritage, and I will be his God and he shall be my son.

(Revelation 21:1-7)

Revelation 21:1-7 | *A New Day Coming*

Remember Cass Elliott, of the Mamas and the Papas? The portly lady had a great song, "There's a New Day Coming," in which she sang about a new order of things, "just around the bend." The markings of this new day, said the song, were peace, joy and love. In the face of today's He-Man and Rambo, this may sound hokey. But to *this* flower-child of the Sixties, the virtues extended were real. The song is over, but the melody remains.

Saint John the Divine was exiled to the island of Patmos for his radicality. Some said he was dangerous. Most dismissed him as just a nut. But in his exile, he received a Divine Revelation of the triumph of peace, joy and love as shown in the unfolding and permanent Kingdom of Jesus Christ.

John's Revelation concludes with a description of the Holy City spilling out of heaven "like a bride dressed to meet her husband."

Weddings, whether earthly or celestial, call for readiness and preparation. I suspect that you two can attest to that! Not only are there special tasks of preparation such as deciding what to wear, the time and place of the service, and what we could eat — there are emotional preparations, too.

Persons rarely fall in love with a stranger "across a crowded room." Those sort of "enchanted evenings" are best reserved for fantasy. The readiness for love in a real sense depends upon a willingness to see and be part of the New Day!

__________ and __________, you are here before us to announce that you've prepared a New Day. Whatever has happened in the Old Day — and I hope that the Old Day was rewarding and pleasant — shall be refined and perfected and made better. That's as it should be, for you have come here with a vision. Included in your vision are elements of a peaceful home, where you can find safety from outside agendas, and put your feet by the fire — a blessing of family, where happy support and the excitement of growth prevail; a security of emotion, where you may say pretty much what's on your mind (if you do it kindly) without fear of it coming back to haunt you.

"Pastor," you say, "you must be a romantic dreamer!"

Well, I am.

And reading this final Word of the Bible seems to bear out this kind of dreaming. The God who is First and Last can be trusted. He has announced an ultimate triumph over death, grief, crying and pain.

But, __________ and __________, there will be days when the Old Order seems yet very much alive! You should know that even though your hearts are warm and festive today, there are wintry days to come. When the car won't start, or the bacon doesn't fry, you'll remember that not *everything* is perfect!

So don't forget the Old Day, where you've come from. Don't forget the poignancy of being alone. Or the loneliness of being your own boss. That way, you'll treasure each other even more!

There *is* a New Day coming, when righteousness will prevail — and a service of marriage creates a brand new home! God lives with his people, and his royal city spills out of the heavens as radiant and permissive as a bride.

Celebrate your marriage, and all that is good.

And keep looking for that which is "just around the bend" — Coming in Peace. Coming in Joy. Coming in Love.